COPPER WOMAN

And Other Poems

Jamaica Kincaid writes, "My mother died at the moment I was born, and so...there was nothing standing between myself and eternity." If place of origin sources story – and connection to origin has almost been destroyed – a writer has nothing standing between herself and eternity. It is from here that Afua Cooper calls forth remnants of story that still recognize their names: her family and ancestors in Jamaica; African, Islamic, Greek, Voudou, Egyptian, and Indigenous Caribbean divinities; historical Black Canadian voices of Richard Pierpont and Marie Joseph Angelique; and "Africa wailin/as Toronto get hot/an Black people dance/communally." Eloquent and visionary, Cooper's poems are like the fruits and flowers her mother sells in the market: "she does not solicit customers/they come of their own volition."

– *Betsy Warland, poet and professor of creative writing, Simon Fraser University, British Columbia*

COPPER WOMAN

And Other Poems

AFUA COOPER

NATURAL HERITAGE BOOKS
TORONTO

Published by Natural Heritage / Natural History Inc.
P.O. Box 95, Station O, Toronto, Ontario M4A 2M8
www.naturalheritagebooks.com

Library and Archives Canada Cataloguing in Publication

Cooper, Afua
Copper woman : and other poems / Afua Cooper.

ISBN 1-897045-09-3

I. Title.

PS8555.O584C66 2006   C811'.54   C2006-901177-X

Front cover: Honolulu Academy of Arts, Gift of Mr. and Mrs. Philip E. Spalding,
1932 (49.1). Diego RIVERA (1886-1957), Mexico, *Flower Seller*, 1926;
oil on canvas, 36 x 43-3/4 in. (91.4 x 111.1 cm).

Back cover: The author, photograph by Edward Gajdel © 2006.

Cover and text design by Sari Naworynski
Edited by Jane Gibson
Printed and bound in Canada by Hignell Book Printing of Winnipeg

Natural Heritage / Natural History Inc. acknowledges the financial support of the
Canada Council for the Arts and the Ontario Arts Council for our publishing
program. We acknowledge the support of the Government of Ontario through the
Ontario Media Development Corporation's Ontario Book Initiative. We also
acknowledge the financial support of the Government of Canada through the
Book Publishing Industry Development Program (BPIDP) and the Association for
the Export of Canadian Books.

It is with profound love and affection that I dedicate this book to my mother, Ruth Campbell Cooper, the original Copper Woman.

TABLE OF CONTENTS

Poet Lights a Natch of Flaming Words

Poet Afua Cooper draws from her wide knowledge of history – personal and monumental – to evoke the ancestors, vistas of her childhood, memories of family and powerful passion in this new book of poetry, *Copper Woman*. The colour red appears in many forms – energy, passion, blood, violence, love, fire, lightning storm, rage and roses. Like the red-brown metal, copper, Cooper's poetry is malleable in each stage of her journey manifested in the five sections of the book – Bird of Paradise, Copper Woman, Biography, Africa Wailin and Black Madonna. The poems capture her thoughts on the divine feminine and her belief that sexuality can be intensely spiritual and therefore has healing potentials.

We meet the poet's family as she pays tribute, remembering qualities that were passed on to her which sustains her. The evocation of life in Westmoreland, Rae Town, St. Thomas and events like the protest against the banning of Walter Rodney in Kingston, Jamaica, are quite visceral. In the poem, "Birds of Paradise," her mother "...invokes the sun to rise," and the poet describes herself as someone whose "words poured from my mouth in flaming chants." It is the symbolism of these "flaming chants" that herald us to the literal flames that burnt down most of Montreal in the poem, "Confessions of a Woman Who Burnt a Town." Cooper's poems incorporate history and urgent contemporary issues – Richard Pierpont, Canadian soldiers in Afghanistan, child soldiers, Palestine, mining of diamonds in Africa, gun violence in Toronto.

In this book, you are sure to meet the Copper Woman as love goddess, seer, vengeful warrior, gifted healer, fecund feminine, earth mother, suffering mother, grieving lover and empowered ruler. She invites Horus to come as "a singer of songs or a weaver of words, a poet...," and to be her lover. She is also a member of the secret guild of Chango, the oracle of Delphi and a lover who engages in an intimate discourse.

Following in the footsteps of her earlier work, *Memories Have Tongue* (1992), Afua Cooper lights the wick of incendiary words that will engulf readers to read, ruminate and remember these poems. Here is a book of poetry that truly embodies the myriad work of one of Canada's most talented and versatile poets, Afua Cooper.

Neil Armstrong, Literary Critic, Toronto

ACKNOWLEDGEMENTS

The poet wishes to thank the Ontario Arts Council and the Toronto Arts Council for their financial support.

PART I

BIRD OF PARADISE

BIRD OF PARADISE

At dawn my mother stands on the hill
behind our house
and invokes the sun to rise
then she goes to the outdoor kitchen
and prepares cassava bread and cocotea for our breakfast

My mother sells fruits and flowers in the market
stuff she grows with her own hands
she does not solicit customers
they come to her of their own volition
and at the end of each day
her items are all sold out

Now at age 42 my mother decides to stop having children
but not because her blood has ceased
"I have peopled the world with the numerous men
and women that my body has birthed," she says
"Now it's time for me to birth other things"

When my mother's back and feet grow tired
so I anoint them with coconut oil
her feet a detailed map
her back the star apple tree outside our front door

My mother has never travelled abroad
but she knows tales of everyland
she says the flowers in her gardens
especially the ginger lily, orchids,
and the bird of paradise, bring her such tidings

My mother is short in stature
her children tower above her
some do not recognize her
or acknowledge her
as they pass by in the market
they are ashamed of this fruit and flower woman
this woman who fed them fish soup and roast breadfruit
that made them so strong
sometimes they mock her
"She looks like something out of a Rivera mural," they jest
but my mother does not hear
her ears are beyond their words

In the evening when she grows weary
my mother sings lullabies to the sun to entice it to sleep
so the dark can come and we can be rejuvenated
"It's in the darkness that we grow strong," she tells us

How wise she is
this woman with a life that no one can capture
how essential she is
this woman who makes gardens flower
and who feeds us milk and corn bread
I watch her as she descends the hill to the marketplace
her skirt at her knee
her black hair flecked with grey

AT THE CENTRE

Today doves flew from my head
and my hair grew
the longing is gone from my body
and I'm filled with peace, perfect peace

No longer shall I speak of electrocuted poets
or the ones who inhaled gas until
they danced in the dizziness of death
but of brown women
who turn the soil with their hands
making vegetable gardens and tending fruit trees

Today I went into my storehouse
selected the choicest oil and anointed my body
wrapped myself in the rarest cloth
of a deep wine red
stood at my front gate
and words poured from my mouth in flaming chants

Today the craftsman has come
to make a design for me
of a woman sitting in deep repose
with doves flying from her head
He has made all the pieces, and they fit
well together
I shall hang it at my window for all the world to see

DUB FOR LISA

(For Lisa Carter who transcended her physicality on October 31, 2003)

A great soul left the earth today
a woman's whose tread was a thunderous buffalo
a woman whose vision ranged high and low
a woman whose words blazed a hundred fires
beneath a blue black sky

This woman you know was fierce
with bare hands she ripped the bars
from a prison cell
and set the captive free
I say she set the captive free
then she rode on a sunray to the ivory tower
released the knowledge
started a people's college

Lisa was an instigator
a teacher
a troublemaker
an initiator
a conspirator
a warrior
a healer
a firebrand
weakheart quake when she utter

Some say she passed too soon
but I say she was ready
Beings wearing garments of light
stood at her front door and called her name
and she consented to go

No
it was not her illness
whether of the mind or flesh
it was just that she was tired
tired of earth and its tedious repetitions
tired of earth and its violent incarnations
so she commanded her heart "Cease"
go meditate on the great peace
woman, find your sweet release

So one evening
Lisa set sail
in the indigo air
in a Ra-powered boat
singing the songs of the sphere

A bright soul left the earth today
a bright soul flew from earth today
bright soul
bright soul
bright soul

Grandmothers carried loads on their heads
babies in their arms
men in their hearts
cut sugarcane until their palms became calloused and bruised
their backs bent, necks stiff, spines misshapen and a permanent hurt
lodged itself in their shoulders
grandmas want to lay their burden down
by the riverside

Grandmothers now lose all dem teeth
but in their mouths are dutty tuff stories
making bread outta stone stories
and stories of how they made it to the other side
of how time pass
an di children grow
an di men die
an the hurt ease
as evening brings with it a purple peace

Now
grandmas sit by their doorstep gazing out onto the street
smoking their pipes
seated in themselves
oracling the scene

HORUS OF MY HEART

My warrior
You are the great magus
Horus, with his far-seeing eye
who make the way clear for me again
Sometimes you come, a singer of songs
or a weaver of words, a poet
and you give me songs, poems, words
as gifts, offerings

Then you appear as my lover
smelling of clove, mint and coriander
and though you are shy, you are bold
enough to touch me, hold me
and when you touch me I cry
because you bring the love of the world
and my heart opens
Oh my wild wonderful man
you have brought me that which I craved
even before I was formed in my mother's womb
and searched for all my life
you brought me such a healing love
that I am not afraid to discover the geography
of your soul, mind and body
and when I do our hearts sing together
and like me you cry, your tears
making fertile the whole earth
from dry, parched, stubborn soil bloodred roses bloom

Oh my wild wonderful man
rivers sing your name
and the birds in their flight echo

it again and again
your eyes are a million moons
the moss-covered stone, durable and soft, your heart
When you dance the whole world trembles and shakes
and when your sing your voice
reaches the four corners of the earth
and every living thing stands still and listens
raging rivers form from your breath
and with one glance barren trees bear fruit

You were not afraid of me
when I revealed my dual countenance
my moon face waxing and waning
you did not look away
yes, you stood in awe
but you thanked me and asked me to teach
you more about myself
And I held you and we danced together
and our love brought forth a new and fresh creation
How strange it is!
All my life you were right there under my nose
waiting patiently, and I didn't see you
so busy was I chasing after the gilded ones

How wondrous it is to know you at last
to be your beloved/soulmate
your equal
your sister
your counsellor
your Bastet*
You first showed up in my life in dreamtime
in nights of triple midnight
when the earth weaves a potent magic

and in my dreams you promised
to cross the border and come to me
My love, the portals of my heart are now wide open

Enter

---

* One of the major divinities in ancient Egyptian religion and lore, and a consort
of Horus.

FOR NUR

I pray for the spirits of the ancestors
known and unknown
for those who died when their homes were burnt and destroyed
for those who were captured in slave raids
for those who died on the march to the coasts
for those who died in the slave castles
for those who died while crossing the sea
perishing at the bottom
for those who died upon arriving, from
diseases
the lash of whip
malnutrition
and of broken hearts
for those who died fighting for freedom
carrying the flame of revolt in their hands
and those, like Nanny, Harriet, Toussaint and Amina, rose up
    triumphant
the spirits of the old one
ever watchful
guiding...
I pray for the spirits of the ancestors
known and unknown

NEGRO CEMETERIES

(Inspired by the Old Durham Road Negro Pioneer Cemetery near Priceville, Ontario.)

"Negro" cemeteries are surfacing all over Ontario
ancestors rolling over
bones creaking
skeletons dusting themselves off
dry bones shaking in fields of corn

A man walks on his farm
the morning after a thunderstorm
see broken headstones a push troo di earth
he rub di mud off
see the inscriptions
like hieroglyphics
reveal names, dates, ancestry
the local museum seh
is an old "Negro" cemetery

All over Ontario
"Negro" cemeteries are surfacing
ancestors rolling over
from the fur trader to the Loyalist to the mariner from Dominica
demanding we remember them
insisting we reveal their history
All over Ontario
ancestors are rolling over
appearing in potato fields
appearing in fields of corn
appearing in wheat fields

Like Osiris, ancestors burst from the earth
in green resurrection

African skeletons shaking the dust from their bones
skulls with rattling teeth
reciting litanies of ancient woes
tongues spouting where none existed before
speaking in funereal language
Griots rising from graves
recounting the stories of their journeys
hafiz tongues uncleaving
reciting surahs of the dawn
babalawos emerging from the storm
divining with their shells and stones
drummers advancing
playing the talking drums
the bata drum
the djembe
the kete and funde
sending messages across this land
loas coming out of their secret place
breaking the shackles of their confinement
Toussaint rising from his dungeon tomb
prophesying blood and fire

Papa Damballah hissed his displeasure at his long internment
Ogun squats, ready with his cutlass
he sniffs the air, scenting signs*

And a woman named Dorinda sits on her tomb
a pipe smoking from between her lips
as she recites and recites and recites the stories of her many passages
the stories of her many transformations

---

* Damballah and Ogun are deities from the Voudou pantheon.

THE CHILD IS ALIVE
(Inspired by the birth scene in the Haile Gerima film, Sankofa.*)*

And a niece of granny Nanny
an Akan woman, a woman who can see far,
a woman with the knowledge of herbs
a woman who works in the field, cutting cane
a woman who speaks the language of her grandmothers
a woman who tells stories of magical animals, of talking trees, and
      of fabled cities beneath mighty rivers
a woman who was stolen from her village when she was 14
a woman who was raped on the slave ship by a white sailor
a woman who flies to Africa when she sleeps

This woman, this niece of granny Nanny
takes her cutlass and runs with the swiftness
of Sogolon Conde in her guise as Buffalo woman*
This woman runs with her machete
an ancient chant rising from her throat
an ancient chant imploring the God and all the
spirits that attend women in childbirth to come
to her aid
She calls her companions, "Form a circle around the dead woman
breathe, breathe deeply, give her breath,
give her life"

This woman, this niece of granny Nanny enters
the circle and with her cutlass, the ancient chant leaping from her lips,
cuts open the belly of the woman and releases the child
while her companions hum and chant softly

Oh praise to the ancestors!
the child is alive

oh Onyame, take the spirit of the mother**
praise to the ancestors,
in the midst of misery and pain
in the midst of humiliation and grief
in the midst of this inhumanity
praise to the ancestors the child lives
oh Onyame, take the spirit of the mother

This woman, this niece of granny Nanny, this ancient midwife
dances with the child, backward, forward, sideward
spins and joins her companions dancing
like the priestess she would have been
had not slavers stolen her away
from her people
The woman dances
east
south
west
north
she holds the child up to the sky
blessings

Oh praise to the ancestors
the child lives
oh Onyame, take the spirit of the mother
oh praise to the ancestors
the child is alive!
Woye! woye! woye!

---

* Sogolon Conde, mother of the Emperor Sundiata Keita of the Empire of Mali
(13th Century), was also known for her ability to change form from human
to animal.

**Onyame is the Twi (Akan language) for God.

PART II
COPPER WOMAN

COPPER WOMAN
(La Mujer de Cobre)

I sit and wait for you
in this long black night
on a slope of this Sierra Maestra
I hear the sound of the sea
I tell it to guide you to me
the night is cold
I cover myself with the red silk shawl
you gave me when we first wedded each other
I shelter our love in my womb
protecting it from
the threat of capture
of being hounded by dogs
of being beaten, killed
or sold, or strangled
of being castrated
I shiver in the dark cold air
when will you come?

I sense your presence, I smell you
your sweat
your breath
your sex
the moon glides from beneath a forgiving cloud
and the light illuminates the bracelets
on my wrists
copper and brass
I remember when you courted me
you laughingly promised to build for me
a palace of brass
but instead gave me a dozen bangles to adorn my arms

Our women wear copper for love
or to draw the poison from the blood
to heal the joints and make them supple

You turn a corner, I stay in the shadow, still unsure
You softly call me by the nickname you gave me
"my copper woman,"
we had agreed on this rendezvous
you take the bancra from your head
and lay this bounty at my feet
roasted breadfruit, dried fish
parched corn, yams,
cassava bread, and an assortment of fruits
You also present me a jug of ginger beer
and a whole side of goat, roasted

I am thankful for the food
but even more grateful to see you
you had gone for days
gone from our mountain hideout
to trade on the plantation below

Feeling safe now, you play with the bracelet on my wrists
telling me what kind of copper each one is made of
the moonlight also illumines our complexion
we have the same kind of ebony
we rub our wrists together
and I feel the sweetness in my lower abdomen

I hold you close to my belly
and find comfort in the regular rhythm of your breath
I rib my nipples against your chest
and you run your fingers along my spine

unknotting the fear
your kiss is warm honey
This moment is perfect and complete
our love will go from everlasting to everlasting

RED EYES

You present me with a bracelet of pure copper
I tell you I cannot accept this gift
because I am thinking of another

Once upon a time
you would have killed a ferocious animal
presented its heart to my family
and then demand my love
but now is present time
and we live hemmed in by wild beasts

Though it is true that we live freely
in our maroon city
we know that hourly
the whites plan
our destruction

Yes, I am thinking of another
months ago he too gave me a gift of copper
he is a blacksmith, a welder
he works with metal and fire
and his eyes are always red

MAROON MAN

They say my grandfather, Silas Stewart
went to St. Thomas to look for work
because there was none in Westmoreland
he left his wife and ten children
and his two mistresses with their five children
between them

But later I learnt (from the mouth of his oldest daughter)
that it was not the lack of work that caused him
to flee the West with such urgency
he ran because there was a machete fight
between him and another man
about a pretty woman

He came home drunk and bleeding
told his wife he had to leave
(his mistresses found out later on)
and caught the first truck leaving for Kingston
he disappeared from the West
He came back fifteen years later to bury his wife
and make acquaintance with his grandchildren

His visit coincided with the year of my birth
It is reported that he looked at me, winked his eye
kissed my forehead with his gray moustache
and spewed me with the rum he was drinking
At six months old, over the protestations of my mother
and the obvious disapproval of my father
he fed me roasted meat
for good luck he gave me a silver threepence

NOMAD'S BLOOD

There's a trumpet in my soul
that blares your name at 3:33 in the morning
as my heart wonders where in the world you are
and my lips silently curse the nomad's blood
that runs in your veins

ATABEYRA
(Mater Dolorosa)

Atabeyra*
Great Mother of the Tainos
Mistress of all moving waters
Lady of Childbirth
Moon woman

Night and day you drift on the foam of the Caribbean Sea
drifting from Florida to the Guianas
tearing your long hair
in grief for your lost children

Atabeyra
you stand on the tallest peak of Seville mountains**
straining your eyes over the vast expanse
of the Carib Sea looking for your lost children
Isis searching the world over for Osiris
Demeter mourning her loss of Persephone
Ishtar weeping for Tammuz
Mary grieving for Jesus
and Yemaya lamenting for Shango

Atabeyra
in your mind's eye you can see your children
making canoes
pounding dried cassava
playing ballgames
swimming
and shamans making sacred ceremonies
and calling on your name
and the names of Yocahu and Opiyel Guaobiran

and we know that when women want children
a safe pregnancy and delivery
they invoke only your aid

Ataybeyra
draw near
come, let me plait your hair
listen, though your children may be gone
gone, gone to the overworld, to Coyaba
if you sit still and listen carefully
you will hear their voices
in the wind and waves of the ocean
if you look intently you will see them walking swiftly
through the cassava patches

You should know Atabeyra that they are not dead
so please my Lady weep no more

Atabeyra
Great Mother of the Tainos
Mistress of all moving waters
Lady of Childbirth
Moon woman

---

*Atabeyra was the Great Mother Goddess of the Taino people, one of the indige-
nous people that Columbus met when he arrived in the Caribbean. The Tainos
eventually were wiped out by the Europeans.

**Mountains in northern St. Ann, Jamaica.

MY NAME IS PHILLIS WHEATLEY*

I was named after a slave ship
named after my master and mistress

I, a frightened eight-year-old girl
lost in this new world
where the ancient names of my ancestry
had no meaning in this country

"Phillis," my master said
"your name is Phillis...
after the ship that brought you here
and Wheatley, my dear
that is...after me...and Susannah"

Could I a young child dared to say
"that's not my name"
that I came from lineages as old as the sun
and I did not want this name of Boston?

I could not say a word
I simply stood and stared
but my ears had heard
and my heart burst in tears

The thought resounded in my head
named after a slave ship? a slave ship?
that vessel that robbed me
of my life and family

That's not my name
I come from people with names as sacred as the sun
and I do not want this name of Boston

Phillis Wheatley
Not Penda Wane or Aminata Coulibaly
not Asta Diallo or Fatou Mandiaty

I wanted to scream and shout
but my tongue lay dead in my mouth
yet this man and wife
seemed to want to preserve my life

So I closed my eyes and nodded my head
thought of my father and then said,
"Yes master, my name is Phillis Wheatley."

---

* Phillis Wheatley, the first Black person in North America to write a book,
Poems on Various Subjects: Religious and Moral, published in England in 1773.

FIRE WOMAN

My aunt cook for men who work on the site
and in the makeshift kitchen
she turn live coal wid her hand
with deft fingers, snatch fry fish from hot oil
a member of the secret guild of Chango*

When she smoke she turn the fire in her mouth
an puff away hard labour
di men dem nevah like it
say a woman shouldn't do dat
dem nevah know she was the oracle at Delphi

---

* Chango is the God of Thunder and Fire in the Orisha tradition.

FIRE WOMAN II

Old women
(perhaps from Dahomé)
crept into my house dressed in robes of crimson
and breathe upon me their breath of fire
they took charge of my house,
painted its walls red
(this caused the unwanted occupants to flee).
Then they gave me a fire bath
(said it would make me invincible)
For my sustenance, they fed me grapes
(from Mary's vineyard)
the juice of which warmed my blood
and caused me to utter in scarlet tongues
For my birthday, they gave me live coals
then changed my name to Ruby

PART III

BIOGRAPHY

BIOGRAPHY

I wonder if anyone will write a biography of me
would they say
that I had visions of becoming a poet
and dreams of writing history
or that my father was a mechanic with gentle eyes

Will they remember that I came from a rural womb
where as an infant I was rocked to bed by the laughter
of rivers that flowed beside our house
Or that I was surrounded by graves of ancient ancestors
and one in particular sat on her grave every morning and waved to me
and I would say "Morning"
Once my mother asked me who I was talking to
and I asked her if she did not see the lady sitting on the grave
with a pipe in her mouth
and my mother commanded me not
to talk back to the lady
and after that she disappeared from her grave

Will they write that my mother's father's people
were Maroons from Trelawny and St. Elizabeth
who walked to Westmoreland
and settled there because they received a dream
telling them to do so?

Will they know that when I was eight
I moved to Rae Town, Kingston
and there it was the sound of sea waves that lulled me to sleep

That every Saturday evening
we feasted on fry fish
chocolate tea

and thick dumplin'd red soup
that you ate with a fork
and heard the sound of Sonny's bike roaring down the street
as he went visit his children's mother

That the first boy I loved
had the face of a Chinese Buddha
and we used to play doctor and patient every evening after school
then I learned of a man named Walter Rodney
whom the men who play ludo at my uncle's shop
said was a communist
and the government deported him
and Kingston rioted

Will they know
only my public face and say
she was a feminist
a Pan Africanist
political activist
cultural worker
educator
rabble rouser
troublemaker

Or will they know that all my life
I've struggled whether to spend my life in solitude and prayer
and that the age of fourteen I sat on the Dome of the Rock
and dhikred with Muhammad

That now my greatest joy is to walk by the river
of Humber
and observe the russet autumn leaf
as it surrenders to the earth

Will they know about the days when I wake up
and want nothing of this world
and its mania
its dementia
its success
its respectability
but would rather whirl within the silence of myself

Will they know that even though I was not Catholic
I still entertained thoughts of becoming a nun
but also wanted seven sons
(I had only one)
that at his birth my breasts were swollen with milk
enough to feed a nation
and I was content
knowing that I had accomplished
the most perfect thing

Will they know
that my mother's sisters
initiated me into earth's mysteries
then sent me into the world
with grace, humour, honesty, and a smile
but most of all, with a sturdy heart

Will they write about these things
or will they only remember that
my father had gentle eyes
and I inherited them

EID AL ADHA, 1995

The women's section
babies wailing
speaking in tongues
children sleeping
dreaming
cotton candy
The women's section
scarlet
violet
disquiet
a riot
of colours

The men's section
solemn
order
a litany of prayers
sacred language
whites robes
black robes
monotone

My daddy fathered many children
and did his best to care for them
He, you know, started to care for himself
at an early age
went out to work at 15
though his mother wanted him to take
the school leaving certificate
but could not afford it

went to work at 15
and to get to the factory on time
for work he would get up at four a.m.
and walked the many miles

And what a good worker he was
42 years at the same place and never late or sick
till a stroke cut him down at age 57

He was a rooted man
never wanted to migrate
though he got plenty opportunities
never wanted to go to the white people's country
he always said it was better to be poor and black
in your own country

What were his dreams?
did he dream of becoming a schoolteacher,
an engineer, a cricketer?
or did he feel totally downpressed by so many children?

The last time I saw him—
through an airplane window—

he was standing on the gallery
waving, hoping that I'd see him
he'd arrived late to see me off
as I go to the white people's country

Now I think of his life
the early death of his father
his struggling childhood
and the sacrifices his mother and aunts made for him

I never knew him young
but I recall him being playful
playing with us, playing ball with us
playing cricket with us
teaching us to read
teaching us the patterns of the sky
teaching us to read the clock
teaching us to tie our shoelaces
He knew so much but said so little
his head bursted with unsaid words
which scattered like the stars
making patterns in the sky

CHILDBIRTH

You demand your place in history
to work out your karmic destiny
your voice, like fire, chatting in my head
insisting, cajoling, demanding
your incarnation

You hide around corners
and assail me as I pass by
you state your mind
in no uncertain terms

At nights you creep
into my dreams
hiding yourself beneath a cabbage leaf
or appearing like a baby animal
telling me I am your mother
ah, you never give up

When I try to explain to you that
in this materiality
things are not as grand and good
as you would like to believe,
you throw back your head and laugh
telling me you've been here many, many
times before and you know your way around

When I say I'm not ready for any more children
you smile and say
"just try me"
I tell you to leave my dreams and go away

Then you start to send me poems and songs
through the mail
and when I answer the phone it's your
voice saying hello and singing me
melodious chants
once you even gave me an idea for a short story

I felt my resolve weakening
one evening as I took a walk in the park and
looked up into the sky and
saw you rowing a boat to meet the night
You waved down to me

I caved in
I gave up
when I saw you on my bed one Sunday morning
feet in the air
and chanting in an ancient tongue
from your last kushitic incarnation

MOTHERHOOD

Of baby bottles
and pumpkin soup
of dettol, lysol and oatmeal soap

DI APPLE OF HAR Y'EYE

Wen mi madda seh mi miserable
an mi faada ignore mi
an mi sista seh mi ugly
an mi bredda call mi mawgah pickney
an everybady tink seh mi is di worse likkle gal
inna di worl
an mi tink nobady love mi
    den mi granny
    mi only granny
come fi mi an comfat mi
she put mi in har lap
an kiss up mi face
she call mi har mango
har punkin
har dumplin
di apple of har y'eye
an tell mi seh mi is di prettiest pickney
she evah know
an how she love mi so
an a feel betta

EVEN WARRIOR WOMEN

Even warrior women sometimes have to don
dresses of green silk
and put away, for a while at least, their martial garb
Even warrior women
sometimes have to cease listening to Artemis' songs
and listen to the silver chants
of the young griot woman in love

Every warrior woman knows that the moon is her guide
and she loves to commune with her
when she is full of blood
But even warrior women know there comes a time
when it's the first moon full of silver light
that she has to sing to
Warrior woman walking down the road
in shoes her feet are not used to
knows she'll wear them for some time
because the martial rhythms have been subdued
and now she walks to a different beat, for a while at least

RICHARD PIERPONT, REVOLUTIONARY SOLDIER
(a poem in three voices)

Revolutionary soldier
revolutionary soldier
revolutionary soldier
Revolution.

Richard Pierpont
revolutionary soldier
at age 77 is no longer in his vigour
and his only wish is for His Majesty's government
to grant him the means to return to his native settlement
so he writes to the king's governor
this July 1821 letter

The petitioner
Richard Pierpont
now of the town of Niagara
a man of colour
a native of Africa
and an inhabitant of this province
since 1780
most humbly sheweth

That your Excellency's petitioner
is a Native of Bondou in Futa
that at the age of sixteen I was made prisoner
sold as a slave, conveyed to America
in the year 1760
bought by a British officer
served the king during the War of Revolution
in the corps called Butler's Rangers

and again during the War of 1812
in a corps of colour
raised on the frontier of Niagara

Revolutionary soldier
revolutionary soldier
stolen from Africa
brought to America
revolutionary soldier
Revolution.

In exchange for my freedom
I have fought your revolution
and raised you new nations
on both sides of the division

That your Excellency's petitioner
is now old and without property
that he has much difficulty
to obtain a livelihood by his labour
that he is above all things desirous
to return to his the land of his mother
that if His Majesty's government be so graciously
pleased to grant him any relief

(You damn thief)

he wished it may be by affording him the means
to proceed to England
and from thence to a settlement
near the Gambia or Senegal region
and from whence he could return to Boudou

(my land of gold)

Because you stole my life
took me from my wife

caused my family strife
stuck in my heart a knife
You cast my people into slavery
you stole the wealth of my country
now give me the reparation
for my overdue repatriation

So please your Majesty
listen to the petitioner's plea
He yearns to return
to the land of his family

Richard Pierpont
revolutionary soldier
said he wrote a letter
to His Majesty's governor

I wish to see again the Senegal waters flow
I wish to see again the water buffalo
gaze at the face of my grandchildren
hold the hands of my brother men

My heart is bursting inside my chest
a prickling pain all through my flesh
a strangulation around my neck
where the slave hunters tied the rope

I still hear the screams of my wife
as the toubab snuffed out her life
and me they tied with ropes and a chain
and took me to this valley of pain

I survived the middle passage
I survived the years of enslavement

58

then I escaped, became a Loyalist
and fought on the side of your government

Now I want to go home to rest
So grant me this last request
Let me die in Futa
face the direction of the Kaaba

Revolutionary soldier
revolutionary soldier
stolen from Africa
brought to Upper Canada
revolutionary soldier
Revolution

DAILY BREAD
(for the Aunts)

My poems come from women talking about blood
and telling me to listen because, soon
I too would experience the bleeding of my moon
and I listen and hear what women do
when their menses are late
and how to unseal their fate
Blue was not only good for whitening clothes on Monday
but also to bring on a woman's blood
another capital remedy was carrot juice
drunk plain

Women talking with ease
as they blow hard on the coal to make it catch
and drop fish into hot oil
the smell of snapper fish frying
as small children stone tamarind fruit from the tree down a gully
and their mothers yell at them to stop stone the tree
because the tamarind still green
and will hurt dem belly

My red wails come from
the hot tar of Kingston streets
and men licking dominoes and ludo on a Rae Town evening
as they argue back and forth
about what they would do to bring on Black liberation
and bwoy, why must Black people must suffer so

Poems come riding on the waves of a Rae Town beach
where we go swimming every Sunday morning
and we di likkle ones stay close to shore
while the big boys

swim out far far
and we ketch wi fraid
cause wi tink dem gwine drown
but dem boys was born fish

St. Michael was not an angel
but a school overlooking the sea
our neighbour was the stone castle of General Penitentiary
and as we walk to school every morning
we watch the prisoners in their white uniforms
sweep the street and plant flowers
and they encourage us, as we pass by, to study our books
and do well in school
But the teachers did tell the boys in our class
that they won't turn out to anything good
but gwine end up inna GP prison
and a few of them did

St. Michael was also the All-Angel church
where I sat every Sunday
comforted by the riddims of songs sung in Latin,
but still unable to experience
the mystery I was supposed to feel

Rae Town was just beginning to lose its glitter
but the Myrtle Bank hotel was still there
and cruise ships still dock in its harbour
and the tree-lined King Street was still majestic
broad avenue and Edwardian architecture
and people could still walk down to the seaside
ketch some cool breeze and dream
and back then it was safe for children to walk by themselves from
    downtown
and go home

Dark-earthed poems emerged from
annual family gatherings in St. Thomas
the land of rebellions
the land of Paul Bogle
the land of Kumina
as my mother's sisters talk right into the night
over fry fish, bammie, and coffee and sometimes shots of
white rum
and they relate over and over again
the flight of their father from Westmoreland
how he went to St. Thomas-in-the-East to look for work
and how he came back and took the older children
and how his wife died
and how they wept
and it broke their hearts to leave the West

My grandfather's daughters
women of slender frame
women very dark of skin
beautiful Yoruba face
with the famous upper lip
that when I see an aunt that I had never seen before
I want to weep because she looks just like my own mother
and they weep when they see me
because they say "Child, your face is just like my father's"
and these women's eyes are coal black with secrets,
which they whisper to each other when they think the children are
    sleeping
and some of them smoke with the fire turned into their mouths
and one could hold her liquor better than any man
and another was a superb dancer
whose husband fell in love with her at a party
and one, of course, was a devout Christian
who had a personal encounter with Christ

And in St. Thomas cousins emerge from every side
and I see the blood flowing between us
tall and straight like our hero grandfather
ebony skin like our nomad ancestor
black with thick coarse hair
eyes bright like a thousand Benin sunrise
and they crown me their princess
a true daughter from their regal ancestry
but since I was a city girl they tek me to the river
and we bathe and ketch crayfish
and make up fire by the riverbank and roast the fish
and later we go to mango bush
and we pick plenty Number 11 and Julie and East Indian

And so in the midst of our meeting
playing
praying
feasting
and loving
these dark-earthed poems emerge
from the blood and bones of our memory

dark-earthed poems
dark-earthed poems
dark-earthed poems
come listen to my rhymes

PART IV

AFRICA WAILIN

AFRICA WAILIN

Stereo-Prophet trow down
at Bathurst and Bloor
an di dj bawl out
"yes, crowd a people
mi seh mi love unu"

Africa wailin
as Stereo-Prophet trow dung
inna downtown
at *Tequila*
an 300 sing as one
sing along wid the dj
sing along wid the singers
wid Sizzla an June Lodge
an Gregory, Tony Rebel,
I love you like fresh vegetable

Africa wailin
as Toronto get hot
an Black people dance
communally
heads up
backs arched
eyes watchin
a far away scene
hands boxin
di air
an feet an hips move
inna kumina, nyahbinghi
as 300 dance together as one

An woman wid dem man rent a tile
body love for a while
love sweet like the waters of the Blue Nile
rub a dub inna different style

An di man wid di hangle
conneck wid di triangle
an di dj leap in di air
a Tutsi dancer
as fire fire
from the Spear
lick him inna him head
an him grab a second mike
hole both a dem a him mouth
an him an Garnet Silk start fi chant it out
Hello Mama Africa
How are you
I'm feeling fine and I hope you're fine too

Woman in weave, red
gold and green
dread wid locks down to dem feet
we all hold hands as we embark
on a journey
as we cross di passage
wid Freddie inna big ship
and Marcia is troddin us to Mt. Zian
for a healin an baptizam

An we help each other as we begin dis passage
weak an tattered
cold and afraid
packed together like sardines in a tin

Lady Saw is embarkin
as Oshun
Burning Spear, di griot from Kangaba
Do you remember the days of slavery?
Do you remember?
Rita Marely an exiled priestess from Kumasi
will start a new world religion
an we love each other
we gentle wid each other
as we continue di journey

An Africa still wailin
an we still crossin
no jobs here in Babylon
is jus pure batterayshan
our men led like sheep into prison
an ours sons lost in whiteness

Africa still wailin
for her children
scattered on white shores
wanderin in di trangle
tryin to find their way home

Woman in red, green, and gold weave
an dread wid locks down to their feet
women in shiny shiny clothes
tight like rass
an men in basic black
wid nuff bling bling
confess their love to each other
as we sing wid the dj
an the singers

songs etched in our memory
songs that live
at the tip of our tongue
songs like
When I see you around a corner
you make me feel like a sweepstake winner
an we look down the street
and see two peace car park
watchin I n I
Ready fi caas shackles pon we again
chains roun wi neck
chains roun wi waists
chains round wi ankles
chains round wi wrist
an as wi fling rockstone
inna Babylon bone
while Africa is still wailin
wailin
wailin
wailin

TRUE REVOLUTION

Revolution in wi heart
revolution in wi thought
revolution in wi house
revolution in di street
revolution widin and widout

No Kamau
there won't be a revolution because
once again they have brought in the colonizers
to whip the people into submission

No Kamau
there won't be a revolution because
artists and other would-be revolutionaries have lost
themselves in the fantasy island of cocaine
and Ilie is no longer the holy herb

No Kamau
there won't be a revolution because
the voice of protest is weak and
punanis rule the airwaves

No Kamau
there won't be a revolution because
gold chains shackle wi necks an minds
while Black miners die (still) in South Africa

Kamau
Your name means (quiet) warrior
and we need warriors like you
fi dance di martial chant

we need Far-I to sound Nyahbinghi drums
we need ones with the spirit of Nanny and Tacky
to plan and strategize
to lay in wait and strike at the enemy
widin and widout

We need fi clean wiself
wi respect wiself
wi respect di female part of wiself
an to know
dat ooman degradation
Black ooman degradation
Black people degradation must stop

We need fi love fi wiself
and wi neighbours
and to know that love indeed is divine
Then Kamau
when all these and more tasks are completed
we will have, oh yes, we will have, we will truly have a Revolution

A revolution in wi heart
revolution in wi thought
revolution in wi house
revolution in d street
revolution widin an widout
revolution 360 degreeeeeeeee

CONFESSIONS OF A WOMAN WHO BURNT DOWN A TOWN
(Inspired by the story of Marie Joseph Angelique*)

I buried the twins that evening
they died of smallpox
were only eight months old
Madame came too to the funeral
and said to me by way of consolation
"C'est la vie,
I too have lost my own."
I went back to work
went back to work in Madame's house
that same evening and at supper she yelled at me
and boxed me full in the face because
I overturned the gravy bowl in her lap

I remember my journey from my island to this island
Rhode Island to Montreal
Lived in Rhode Island all my life till
monsieur came from Montreal on one of his business trips
he bought me because he said I looked like a healthy wench.
Monsieur died soon after and madame never forgave me
but I had nothing to do with it, he died of consumption

The twins died too.
After we buried them that evening
my heart changed position in my chest
and I was seized with one desire and one desire only
and that was to leave the prison of this island
But where could I go
because throughout the whole world
in all the continents people who look like me
were bound

But still, all I could see was
my feet running, no chains, no rope, no shackles
free

Madame talking to her best friend
and confessor Father Labadie
"I'm going to sell that negress, she's getting too much
for me, she's getting too uppity
And furthermore since François died I just can't seem to manage
    too well
Look a buyer for me father, perhaps the church is interested."
I bring in the food and pretend like ah neva hear
and I serve the food good and proper
was on my best behaviour
roll back mi lip and skin mi teeth
roll back my yai and show the white
den I went back to mi room in the cellar
and mek mi plan

Smoke, smoke, too much smoke
only intend fi one house fi burn
fire, fire, too much fire
but it done go so already
and I running
my feet unshackled, unbound,
free
running pass di city limits
while behind me the fire rage
and my raging heart change back into its rightful position

He was running too
an apprentice, from France
I gave him all my food to take me or show me

the way to New England but he tek the food
and leave me while I was sleeping
an the constables caught me

I don't utter a word as I sit here in the jailhouse
Father Labadie come to confess me
but I refuse
their god is not my god
"Arson is one of the worst crime in New France, Marie,"
he say to me, "Confess now and save your soul."
I spit on the ground
outside, the mob want to rip me from limb to limb
but I not afraid, a strange calm fill my body
and I at peace, peace, perfect peace

Guilty, the judge pronounce
and the sentence: to be tortured, my hands cut off
my body burned and the ashes scattered
to the four corners of the earth
I break down, my body crumple in a heap
and before my eyes I see the twins
and they look so alive as if they waiting
for me to come nurse them
The sentence is reduced
Now I am to be hanged only and my body burned
Father Labadie come back for di confession
And I confess
is I Marie who set the fire
I say yes
I start it in madame's house by the river
50 building destroy
the hospital, the cathedral
I confess

is I Marie who burn this city
so write that down Father Labadie
write down my story so it can be known in history
with my heart burning I take the sacrament
and accept the final rites
outside the guard is waiting
to take me to my hanging
outside the guard is waiting
to take me to my dying
outside the guard is waiting
to take me to my burning

Soon I will be free from the prison of this island
and I will fly and fly and fly

---

* In June 1734 Marie Joseph Angelique, a Black slave woman, was hanged in
Montreal for burning down much of that town in April 1734.

DIAMOND IS A GIRL'S BEST FRIEND

Which girl?
The African girl?
The one who lost her pearl?
I don't think so.

Find the biggest diamond in Guinea
But in the same locale and vicinity
children die from common illness
the cure for which cost only a few cents

They tell us that Africa is poor
in truth she is the wealthiest of nations
slice her belly and rob her once more
stealing her gold and diamonds

Dem call this underdevelopment
Centre/periphery arrangement
tell us that is Africa's fault
as dem launch another frontal assault

And diamond is a girl's best friend?
Which girl?
The African girl?
The one who lost her pearl?
I don't think so.

The diamond merchants of Amsterdam
New York
Toronto
Belgium
guzzle the blood of Africans

as Sierra Leone bleeds
and Liberia is in need
Congo is wailing
South Africa is bawling

And diamond is a girl's best friend?

Look at the rock on her finger
see how it sparkle and glitter
Sierra Leone sorrow and slaughter
crafted by an Amsterdam jeweller

De Beers diamonds are forever
seal your love till the twelfth of never
know that the stone you give your lover
comes from the killing fields of Africa

And diamond is a girl's best friend
Which girl?
The African girl?
The one who lose her pearl?
Me no tink so.

AH CAAN TINK ABOUT IT

Ah caan tink about it
ah jus caan tink about it

say i walk down the street feelin depress
tinkin di worl inna mess
ah look at di headlines
and wat do i see
half a million murdered in Kigali

no ah caan tink about it
really caan tink about it

at di bus stop is a bag lady
eatin fram di garbage pan
it could be funny
but it no funny
for it freezin cole
20 below

no caan tink about it
jus caan tink about it
cause if i tink about it
it jus gwine bruk mi spirit

THE STONES ARE SPEAKING
(In three voices)

The stones are speaking
let them speak!
The coconut shells are speaking
let them speak!
The cowries are speaking
let them speak!
The sand is speaking
let it speak!

Lorenzo is bringing down Ifa
to divine a pressing matter
Orunmila sits with his eyes half closed
as he turns the pages of the book of secrets

We sit before Lorenzo and we ask
shall it be tonight
shall we revolt tonight
shall the plains burn with sweet fire tonight
shall all the whites face their doom tonight?
Though our resolve is strong
there is still confusion in our heart

Red shall be the colour of the night
the red of the fire that shall burn the plains
and the red of the blood and anger of humans

Speak to us clearly
We do not understand
throw the shells again Lorenzo, ancient blacksmith from Benin
throw the shells again Lorenzo, you most gifted of diviners

throw the shells agains Lorenzo, knower of the language of the forest
only you can decipher the patterns
throw the shells again Lorenzo
so we may know for sure
Will we have success tonight?

> Many will die
> but that must be
> many will die
> but you shall also succeed

Then tonight we shall make the plains run red with fire
how sweet it shall smell as the cane trees explode
Tonight the whites will wish they had never seen this land
or the face of a Black
Gracias, Lorenzo
Modupe, Orunmila
we shall make our sacrifice now
Ifa has spoken, we are no longer afraid

> The stones have spoken
> So be it!
> The coconut shells have spoken
> so be it!
> The cowries have spoken
> so be it!
> The sand has spoken
> So be it!

CONGO WI COME FROM
(For Ian Cooper)

So di wite bwoy fine out di secret
of di red handerchief
dat wen yuh flash Chango inna im face
im haffi front up di visa
ah mossi one a wi tell him

so dem sen roun a memo to di embassy staff
dat anyone who produce a red kerchief
an wipe him face
even dough the room air condition cool
fi instantly deny him di visa
But im no know seh a Congo wi come from
an if wi really want di visa
wi haffi get it
Im no know seh wi have di powers a di wind
an rain
an lightning,
and tundah,
an smoke behine wi
Im no know seh wi have di powers a di palm,
di silk cotton tree,
eggshell
stones
seashells
sand
and di sea fi work fi wi
Im no know seh wen
wi open wi mout an chant
an invoke
and recite

wi move mountains
wid wi words
So mek im gwan
mek im tink seh im win
mi im gwan
mek im tink seh im know
all wi secret
mek im gwan sit back in im high chair
an stamp "Denied" in di passport
an smile as im do so
Mek im gwan
cause im no know seh a Congo wi come from
an if wi really want it
we haffi getti

KILLED BY "FRIENDLY AMERICAN FIRE" IN AFGHANISTAN

We mourn the death of the four soldiers
today, it is the one from Toronto, the one with the heartical smile
Four men, barely out of their teens,
still waiting to embrace life
still waiting to father unborn children
who now must wait, their journey interrupted, in the void

These men died in a faraway country
a brown country
a country laid bare by war and famine
and these men were there to lay it bare even more

When a life is lost
the universe weeps
and when a life is saved the universe rejoices
many lives have been lost in Afghanistan
the lives of humans and of the earth

As a soldier in a war zone
one expects to die, most likely by the fire of the enemy
but not by the hand of a friend
these men died in "friendly fire"

We train soldiers to kill
and then give them permission to kill for us
and when they kill and return alive and victorious
we give them a hero's welcome
When they come back cold and dead we give them a hero's funeral
with full military salute
We willingly forget the deeds they have done

In ancient Yorubaland
when soldiers come back from war
they are secluded
they cannot be with their families
they cannot marry
they cannot engage in daily intercourses until they are cleansed
until a ritual is performed to wash and cool their heads
their heads full of violence
and their hands full of blood
They have to be cleansed because the citizens
those who send them to kill, maim, and destroy
know that war compromises the spirit
and despoils the soul
So the soldiers are secluded
at a place sacred to Ogun
the deity of war
and their heads are washed by blacksmiths
those who make the instruments of war

Here we give our soldiers a hero's salute
whether in death or life
while we send more
to that brown land and other lands like it
to continue sacrificing humans and the earth

The one from Toronto
Ainsworth Dyer
I study his face
handsome
his smile tells that he is loved

They bury him
his parents,

his sisters
his lover
the Governor General
the police chief
the mayor
the citizens of the town
they mourn and weep
Did they wash his head? I asked myself
I pray for him to enter the afterlife with peace in his heart
I watch it on TV and my tears flow
They lay him to rest at the Necropolis
his unborn child weeps

CHILDREN GONE TO WAR
(A dub for the Child Soldiers)

Children, children
7, 8, 9, 10, 11
I'm talking bout the children

Children gone to war, me seh dat no good
children gone to war in my neighbourhood
children gone to war to maim and kill
children gone to war playing a dirty game

War inna place like Sierra Leone land
war inna place like Lebanon
war inna place like Palestine land
war inna place like Afghanistan

We took them outta school
and gave them a tool
to kill other children
who look just like them

There were girls and there were boys
marching off with their adult toys
some looked bad and some looked sad
but not one ever did look glad

So they went off to war with guns on their backs
they went off to war to launch an attack
they went off to war bombs strapped around their waist
they went off to war blood sprouting from their face

Children, children
7, 8, 9, 10, 11
I'm talking bout the children

in Toronto they say
Come my nigger
Pull dis trigger
Hot boys shoot down each other
in Toronto world-class city
who no dead gone fi life
in the general penitentiary

Children, children
7, 8, 9, 10, 11
We talking bout the children

WOMAN A WAIL

Woman a wail
di eart is in labour
woman a wail
creation in danger
and what shall she bring forth from her travail?

Her mountains shall roar and spit fire
her bowels shall move and cause the eart to split
from one end to another
our minds too shall be rent asunder
this woman shall avenge herself

Who is she that looketh forth as the morning,
fair as the moon, clear as the sun,
but terrible as an army with banners
She wail an bawl
as she destroy but
she create again and again
she wail an shriek
as she bring forth
a new way of thinking
a new way of living
a new understanding
and a new new new creation

From the mouth of the Ganges
from the throat of the Yangtze
from the heart of the Niger
from the belly of the Amazon
she dance
she dance down lightning and thunder

she dance down brimstone and fire
she is a mighty earthquake
she is a non-stop hurricane
she dance
    and
dance
and dance and dance
she dance down lightning and thunder
she dance down brimstone and fire, fire
she is a mighty whirlwin
she is a non-stop volcano, ooh

She dance her dance of terror
she dance her dance of fear
look she dancing on the four winds
dancing the world's end, ooh

Ah seh
woman a wail
the eart is in labour
woman a wail
creation in danger
woman a wa-eh-eh-eh-eh-ail
the eart is in labour

And what shall she bring forth from her travail
what shall she bring forth from her travail?
A new way of thinking
a new way of living
a new understanding
a new way fi si tings
a new way fi do tings
and a new new new Creation

PALESTINE 1993

Women in veil
throwing stones
men in jail
with broken bones
soldiers with uzzi
and other big guns
ready to kill
ready to kick down

women wail
babies cry
grandfathers ask
oh lord why
as soldiers with uzzi
and other big guns
do plenty killing
an nuff kicking down

overcrowded homes
no heat in winter
no running water
old men just satta

sand-drenched roads
become rivers of blood
as a murderous trickle
turn into a flood
soldiers with uzzi
and other big guns
do plenty killing
and nuff kicking down

streets full of garbage
refugee camp
a nation in exile/in bantustan
the star of the desert
no longer shine
on broken dreams that were mine
the star on the desert
can no longer shine
on the broken dreams that were once mine

women in veil
throwing stones
children killed
fighting for a home
soldiers with uzzi
and other big guns
ready to kill
ready to kick down

boys become men overnight
where they learn that
might is right
love is buried
and fear is carried
as soldiers with uzzi
and other big guns
ready to kill
ready to throw down

sticks and stones
broken bones
soldiers with uzzi
and other big guns

do plenty killing
and nuff kicking down
the star of the desert
no longer shines
gunshot shatter dreams that were mine

PART V

BLACK MADONNA

BLACK MADONNA
(for Jimi Hendrix)

All along the evolution
all along the untenable path
I search for my Black Madonna
but she refuse to show her face
I walk the Earth like a nomad
I seek but cannot find
all along the path I trod
(am I?) losing my mind

All along the evolution
all along the untenable path
I search for my Black Madonna
instead I find two unicorns
sharing the same set of horns
and a woman called Maria
who is a shaman, a healer
with them as my companions
I search for the promise
locked between the portals

LOVETALK

My love enwraps you
my love enfolds you
I am the river from which all sweetness flows

My breasts your milkpots
from which you refused to be weaned
my navel your centre

You smell my particular smell
and your whole being begins to quiver
I am the tree of life
the giver of your knowledge

You want to remain forever
in the warmth of my moon glow
to taste its essence and wonder
and its sweetness
I am the river from which all good things flow

MAN OF FIRE

Man of fire
surging wave
your warm breath recites sexy secrets to my neck
your tongue licks my palm
and activates the volcano in my vulva

Man of fire
what pleasures lie in your hand
what nectar on your tongue
what maddening heat in your hips
My wild man
how you come into my life like Ogun
unobtrusive, solitary, without fanfare
I was not aware of you
until you smiled at me
called me "Miss"
that smile
caused an electrical storm to rage
in my soul
I did not become aware of your madness and wildness
until you cupped my breasts in your palms
anointed my belly with midnight kisses
feasted from my honeypot
then rode me on the night wind

Man of fire
your love is as green as the Blue Mountains
solid as the plains of Liguanea
surging like the waves that batter the shore of St. Thomas
cool as the waters of Milk River
hot as a tropical wind

SEASPRAY

Love cause us to behave like children
without consciousness or shame
like me feeding you the flesh of naseberries
and you licking the juice from my fingers
like you licking the seasalt from my skin
from between my toes, behind my ears, behind my knees
in full view of the people on the beach
because you want to keep forever my taste in your mouth

We paddle a canoe to the reef
"Let's row to Cuba," I say
"we will disappear
live in a shack by the sea
have four children
feed them milk, and cornmeal porridge
and bequeath to them
the seaspray
and the moonrays"
and the music, the music

Instead we row to the deserted island
which keeps the reef company
and swim naked in the waters around it
intoxicated by each other's presence and movements
watch Seville mountain standing guard in the distance
and in the western sky the purple hands of twilight
were waiting to escort the sun to sleep
And even though we are miles away from the beach
the music from Sonny's sound system
floats to us on the water
it is Marcia singing "Trodding to Jerusalem"

"Let's spend the night on the island," you suggest
"We would be eaten alive by the sandflies and mosquitoes," I reply
"But think of it," you say
"think of it, here we could cry, and laugh and shout
as loud as we want, in our coming"

BENEATH A FERVENT MOON

You entered my gates
like Shams of Tabriz
and caused me to throw away my books and knowledge
my theories and dogmas
my neat equations

Instead of feeding me soup
you fed me wine
and read my palm beneath a fervent moon

HIBISCUS

You know all my secrets
all the secrets of my body
have knowledge of my love triangle
as hot and sweet as freshly baked cinnamon buns
red as a hibiscus flower

MY ILLUSION

That we run away to Portland
in the mountains
to a place called House Hill
where you can touch heaven with your finger
and each morning awakened by rain drizzling
thru a rainbowed sunlight
there you can stand on your own peak
and see the lighthouse at Port Morant
sending signs to voyagers
and on a clear day
see the outline of Cuba
Oriente, Oriente

Or it could be to Port Antonio
the side where the land juts
into the sea
close to the lagoon
everyday we would feast on mangos and mint tea
and make love in the purple air of twilight

It was in Portland by the Blue Lagoon
that I saw the brightest moon
rise from the black sea
and stride naked across the sky
conquering all with her luminous light

SUGAR

Brown sugar
raw, dark, Demerara
made from thick Barbados molasses
solidified by a Jamaican heat
Come let me eat you
mix you in my lemonade
blend you in my cake mix
stir you in my coco tea
my dark sugar

RED SEA WOMAN
(For X)

In our dreams the masks fall off
and we stand brave and unafraid
our truth burning like the luminous light at sunrise
My dream last night was that I was a bird, a hoopoe
engaged in intimate discourse with you, my Sulayman

That I love you, there is no doubt
and want to wrap myself in your embrace
bless the lids of your eyes with tiny kisses
run my tongue across your throat
reel and stagger from the wine of your intercourse
shiver and shake from the nectar of your kiss
But civilization with its mores and conventions
have blighted our growth
we have become timid and afraid
our wildness corralled liked frightened horses
now we run meekly on this flat terrain

We have turned the jungle into a manicured garden
where only a captured bird lives

Remember when we used to eat Seville oranges
sprinkled with salt from the Swahili coast
dive for pearls in the Red Sea,
bloom roses from the red soil of the Rift valley?
Now here we sit in this city of civilization
drinking second cup coffee

How long shall we continue this banal existence?
If you do not want to leave

I shall go without you
untie the feet of the bird
and let it find its way

MAKING LOVE IN LOTUS POSE

At the line that separates night from day
at the time when dawn begin its stride
over the horizon
accompanied by the fizzle of the stars
as they shoot across the sky
and the shouts of the fishermen
as they bring in their first catch
followed by the drone of the bus on the road
the last crow of the cock
I slip from sleep
and awake to the insistence of your lips on my skin
as you sip from the cup of my thousand-petalled lotus
Gold and rose
the colours of the dream I had

In another time and place
you would have been king
or at least a general in his army
The purple of the morning enfolds us
as we perform this ancient rite
gold and rose
misty blue and violets too
breath and air
fire and lightning
riddim and wail
shooting stars
surging waves
life and death
aaah

If not a general in the king's army
then the principal dancer in the queen's troupe

ABOUT THE AUTHOR

Afua Cooper is an eminent award-winning poet, author, historian, curator, performer, speaker, cultural commentator and recording artist. A recent winner of the Harry Jerome Award for Professional Excellence, she was also chosen by the editors of *Essence* magazine (Oct. 2005) as one of the 25 women who are shaping the world. Afua has been featured in the most recent volume of *Contemporary Black Biography: Profiles from the International Black Community*, a Thomson and Gale publication. She has written four books of poetry, including the award-winning *Memories of Tongue*, and her poems have been widely anthologized in national and international publications. Her poetry has also been recorded on CDs. Her work is rooted in the African-Caribbean tradition of Dub poetry, and she is a founding member of the Dub Poets Collective. In addition, Afua Cooper wrote a number of history texts and essays, including the best-selling *The Hanging of Angelique: Canada, Slavery and the Burning of Montreal*. Holding a Ph.D. in African-Canadian history, Afua currently teaches history at the University of Toronto where she is cross-appointed between the history department and Canadian Studies.